ABOUT THE AUTHOR

Neil Ardley has written a number of innovative nonfiction books for children, including *The Eyewitness Guide to Music*. He also worked closely with David Macaulay on *The Way Things Work*. In addition to being a well-known author in the fields of science, technology, and music, he is an accomplished musician who composes and performs both jazz and electronic music. He lives in Derbyshire, England, with his wife and daughter.

Project Editors Scott Steedman and Laura Buller
Art Editors Christopher Howson and Peter Bailey
Production Louise Barratt
Photography Clive Streeter
Created by Dorling Kindersley Limited, London

Library of Congress Cataloging-in-Publication Data
Ardley, Neil.
The science book of the senses/Neil Ardley.—1st U.S. ed.
p. cm.
"Gulliver books."
Summary: Gives instructions for a variety of simple experiments that explain how the body's five senses operate.
ISBN 0-15-200614-1
1. Senses and sensation—Juvenile literature. [1. Senses and sensation—Experiments. 2. Experiments.] I. Title.
QP434.A73 1992
612—dc20 91-20587

Printed in Belgium by Proost
First U.S. edition 1992
A B C D E

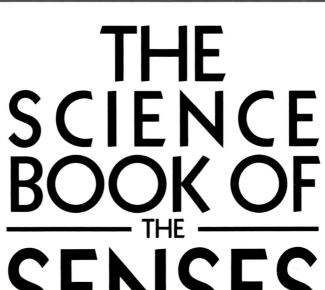

THE SCIENCE BOOK OF THE SENSES

Neil Ardley

HBJ

Gulliver Books

Harcourt Brace Jovanovich, Publishers

San Diego   New York   London

What are the senses?

Your senses are your brain's link to the world you live in. Without your senses you wouldn't be able to hear music or to smell your dinner cooking. You wouldn't know if the air in the room was hot and stuffy or icy cold. You wouldn't be able to see this book or even feel it to turn the pages.

Most of us have five senses: sight, hearing, touch, taste, and smell. They do not always work well. Some people cannot see or hear, for example. But we all use the senses we have to keep in touch with the world around us.

Talking hands
People who lack one sense may use another to help them. Some deaf people communicate in sign language.

Scent sense
Smells are mixed in with the air around you. To identify smells, you breathe or sniff in air to move it past smell detectors in the upper part of your nose.

Play ball!

When you play sports, you use your senses of sight, hearing, and touch. The better you are able to use these senses together, the better you play.

Balancing act

Circus performers depend on their ability to balance. Your senses of sight and touch help you to balance, and your ears have special parts inside of them that tell you which way is up.

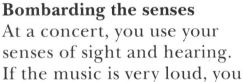

Bombarding the senses

At a concert, you use your senses of sight and hearing. If the music is very loud, you may also feel its vibrations.

⚠ This is a warning symbol. It appears within experiments next to steps that require caution. When you see this symbol, ask an adult for help.

Be a safe scientist

Follow all the instructions carefully and always use caution, especially with glass, scissors, hot water, and sharp objects.

Never put anything into your ears, eyes, mouth, or nose, and be careful when testing yourself or others.

Inside the ear

How do you hear sounds? By making a model of an ear, you will see how your ears change sounds into signals that are sent to your brain. Your brain translates these signals into the sounds you hear.

You will need:

Stiff card

Tape

Modeling clay

Rubber band

Plastic wrap

Cardboard tube

Flashlight

Sheet of paper

The plastic wrap must be tight.

1 Stretch the plastic wrap over one end of the tube. Secure it with the rubber band.

2 Roll the sheet of paper into a cone and tape the edge.

This is your model ear.

3 Insert the small end of the cone into the tube. Tape them together.

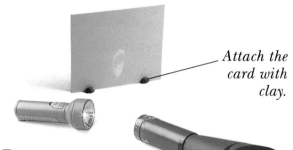

Attach the card with clay.

4 Stand the card on a table. Shine the flashlight on the plastic wrap so that a spot of light reflects onto the card.

5 Shout or sing loudly into the cone. The spot of light vibrates rapidly!

Sound waves make the plastic wrap vibrate back and forth, causing the reflected light to vibrate as well.

The cardboard tube acts like your ear canal. Sounds pass through the opening in your ear and along the ear canal to the eardrum.

The plastic wrap acts like the eardrum at the end of your ear canal. The inner ear changes the eardrum's vibrations into signals that are sent to the brain.

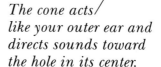

The cone acts like your outer ear and directs sounds toward the hole in its center.

Examining the ear
A doctor uses a special instrument to examine your ears. This device allows the doctor to look down the ear canal to the eardrum.

Lost sounds

Why do you have two ears, one on each side of your head? Find out by covering one ear and trying to tell exactly where a sound is coming from.

You will need:

Two pencils

Cloth

Cover one ear to block out sounds.

1 Use the cloth to blindfold a friend. Then ask your friend to cover one ear with a hand.

We can't find the source of a sound using only one ear.

2 Quietly move around the room. Tap the two pencils together and ask your friend to point toward you. Your friend is usually wrong!

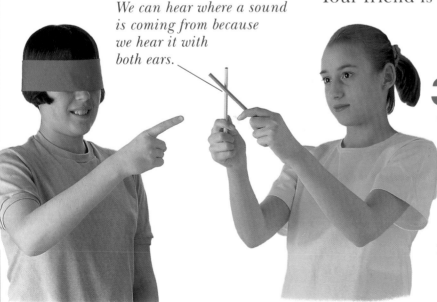

We can hear where a sound is coming from because we hear it with both ears.

3 Ask your friend to try again, but this time using both ears. Now your friend can point to where the sound is coming from every time.

Hot or cold?

Your sense of touch tells you whether things are hot or cold. Or does it? See how the same thing can feel both hot and cold.

Add a little cold water if the hot water is too hot to touch.

1 ⚠ Fill one glass with hot water, and one with cold water and ice. Mix hot and cold water in the other glass.

2 Put one finger into the hot water and another into the ice water. Leave them there for a minute.

3 Dip the hot finger into the warm water. The warm water feels cold, because it is not as hot as your skin.

You can tell only that something is hotter or colder than your skin.

4 Now dip the cold finger into the warm water. The water feels hot!

Touch test

We easily feel things that touch our skin. Nerves in the skin detect them and tell us how hot or soft or painful they are. But how good is our sense of touch?

You will need:

Thick cardboard

Pins

Coloring pens

Cloth

Compass

Scissors

Ruler

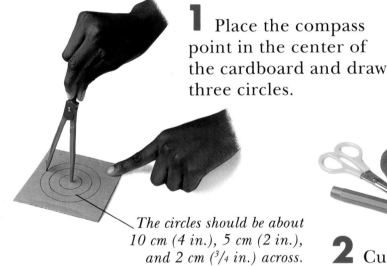

1 Place the compass point in the center of the cardboard and draw three circles.

The circles should be about 10 cm (4 in.), 5 cm (2 in.), and 2 cm (³/₄ in.) across.

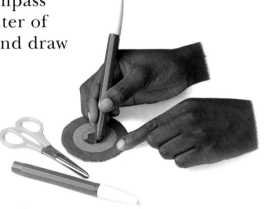

2 Cut out the largest circle. Color the different circles.

3 Blindfold a friend with the cloth.

4 ⚠ Stick two or three pins into the center circle. Make sure that the pinheads are the same height.

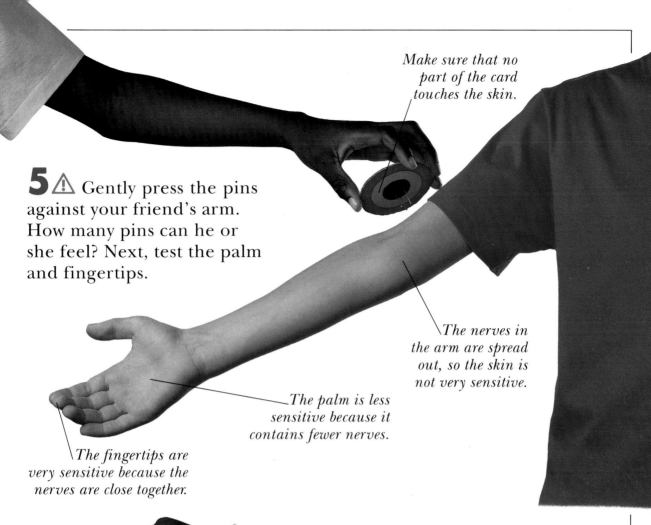

Make sure that no part of the card touches the skin.

5 ⚠ Gently press the pins against your friend's arm. How many pins can he or she feel? Next, test the palm and fingertips.

The nerves in the arm are spread out, so the skin is not very sensitive.

The palm is less sensitive because it contains fewer nerves.

The fingertips are very sensitive because the nerves are close together.

6 Test the arm, palm, and fingertips again with the pins spread around the middle and then the outermost circle. Your friend's arm will only detect all the pins when they are in the outermost circle.

Making music
Playing a musical instrument such as the saxophone requires great sensitivity of touch. Wind instruments are played with the lips and fingertips, which are among the most sensitive parts of the body.

Reading in the dark

Can you read without using your eyes? With the sense of touch in your fingertips, you can read by feeling instead of by sight.

You will need:

Cork tile   Scissors   Map pins   Pen   Cloth

1 ⚠ Cut the cork tile into four squares.

2 Draw a number on each cork square.

3 Stick map pins into the outline of each number.

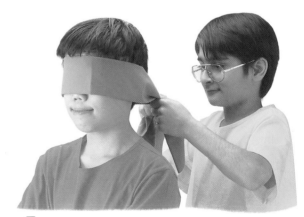

4 Blindfold a friend with the cloth.

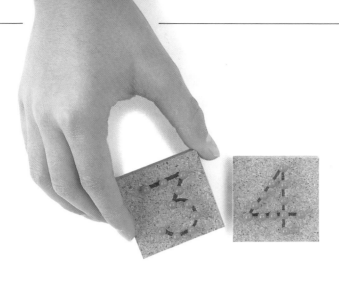

5 Place the numbers side by side on a tabletop.

Your fingertips are very sensitive because there are many nerves in the skin there.

6 Have your friend read the numbers by feeling the shapes with his or her fingertips.

Books for the blind
Blind people read books that are printed in a special alphabet called braille. Each braille letter is a pattern of raised dots. Blind people read by quickly running their fingers over the patterns of dots.

Inside the eye

By building a model eye, you will see how light enters the eye and forms images. A part of your eye changes the images into signals that tell your brain what you are seeing.

You will need:

Tissue paper

Tape

Stiff card

Modeling clay

Flashlight

Scissors

Magnifying glass

Fishbowl full of water

1 Tape the tissue paper to the side of the fishbowl.

2 Use some clay to attach the magnifying glass to the table top. This is your model eye.

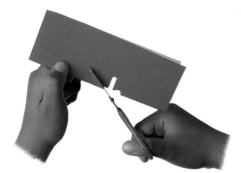

3 Fold the card and cut out half of a figure. Unfold it.

4 Use some clay to stand the card on the table in front of the magnifying glass.

5 Place the flashlight in a straight line with the figure and model eye. Turn it on. An upside-down image of the figure appears on the tissue paper. Move the fishbowl back and forth until the image is sharp.

The round bowl acts like your eyeball.

Your eye has a lens like the magnifying glass that focuses light.

Light from the figure is bent by the magnifying glass and focused onto the tissue paper.

The tissue paper at the back of the bowl is like the retina at the back of the eye, where the image is formed.

When an image forms on the retina, signals go to your brain and you see the object.

Black hole

The dark hole at the center of the eye is the pupil. The pupil changes size to control the amount of light that the lens focuses on the retina. It enlarges in weak light to let more light in, and it shrinks in bright light. This helps you to see more easily.

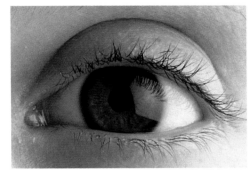

Cat and mouse

Draw a cat and a mouse—then keep the cat from "catching" the mouse. This trick works because each of your eyes has a blind spot. You cannot see any image that falls on that part of your eye.

You will need:

Ruler

Paper

Pencil

Colored pens

1 Make two marks on the paper about 8 cm (3¼ in.) apart.

2 Draw a cat by the left-hand mark and a mouse by the right-hand one.

3 Place a hand over your left eye. Stare at the cat as you bring the paper slowly toward you. The mouse suddenly vanishes. Now try staring at the mouse with your right eye covered. The cat disappears.

Each of your retinas has an area that is not sensitive to light. You cannot see any image that falls there.

Target practice

Why are two eyes better than one? Try to hit a target while covering one eye and find out.

Buttons   Cup

With only one eye, it is hard to tell the true position of your friend's hand.

1 Sit at a table with a friend. Place the cup in the middle of the table.

2 Cover one eye. Ask your friend to hold a button and move it around over the table. Say "Drop!" when you think the button is over the cup. How often do you get it right?

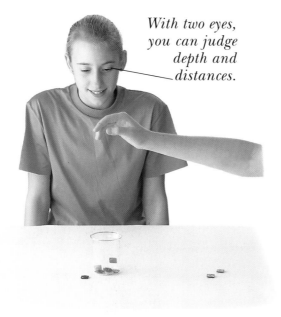

With two eyes, you can judge depth and distances.

3 Try again with both eyes open. Your score will be much better.

Here's looking at you
An owl has two large eyes in the front of its head. These help the owl judge the position of its prey—and then catch it.

Two or one?

Can you trick yourself into seeing two pictures as one? It's easy to do. This works because the eye still sees things for a short time even after they're out of sight.

You will need:

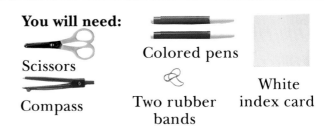

Scissors

Compass

Colored pens

Two rubber bands

White index card

1 Using the compass, draw a circle on the card. Then cut it out.

Make the holes directly opposite each other.

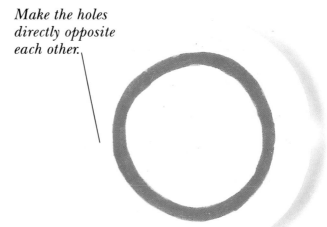

2 Make two holes near the edges of the card. Then draw a circle on one side.

3 Draw a plus sign on the other side of the card.

4 Thread a rubber band through each hole.

5 Flip the card around several times until the rubber bands are tightly twisted.

Your eye continues to "see" an image for a moment after the image has vanished. This is called "persistence of vision."

6 Release the card. While it whirls around, you will see the plus sign inside the circle.

Because the card spins so fast, you see both images at the same time.

Motion pictures

Movies are long strips of photographs, each one slightly different from the one before. A projector flashes these photographs rapidly, one after another, onto a screen. Your brain combines the photographs into one moving picture.

Seeing and believing

Can you always believe your eyes? What if they show you something you *know* is wrong? Make an optical illusion and find out how your brain sometimes makes you see things that aren't there.

You will need:

Compass   Scissors

Three different colored index cards

Pencil

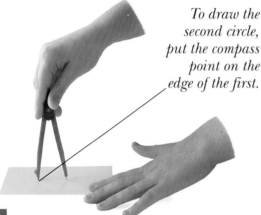

To draw the second circle, put the compass point on the edge of the first.

1 Use the compass to draw two overlapping circles on one card.

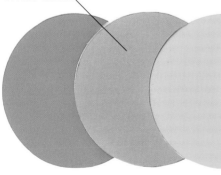

All three crescents should be the same size.

2 Cut out the crescent shape. Trace around it on the other two cards and cut the shapes out.

The green crescent seems wider.

Your brain is confused by the way each crescent curves. They don't appear to be the same size.

3 Place the crescents in a line. Which one looks biggest?

The green crescent seems taller.

4 Change the order of the crescents. Now which one looks biggest?

Reaction ruler

How fast do your senses work? Test your reaction time and find out just how quickly your senses tell you to take action.

You will need:

Six colored markers

Paper

Glue

30 cm (12 in.) ruler

Scissors

Pencil

1 Trace around the ruler on the paper. Cut out the shape and mark six bands, each 5 cm (2 in.) long.

2 Color each band a different color. Then glue the paper to the ruler.

Keep your thumb and forefinger about 1cm (¹/₂ in.) apart.

3 Hold out your hand. Ask a friend to suspend the ruler with the bottom color band between your thumb and forefinger.

4 Have your friend drop the ruler without warning. Catch it! The color you grab shows your reaction time.

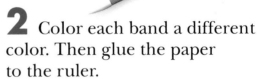

Slow reaction time

Medium reaction time

Fast reaction time

Full of flavor

You can taste many different flavors. But if you test your sense of taste, you will find that it's not just your mouth that tells one flavor from another. Your nose does a lot of tasting, too.

You will need:

Four different kinds of pure fruit juice

Cloth

Large glass of water

Four small glasses

1 Pour each fruit juice into a small glass.

2 Use the cloth to blindfold a friend.

It is easy to recognize each flavor.

3 Have your friend sip the juices one by one and say which juice he or she has just tasted.

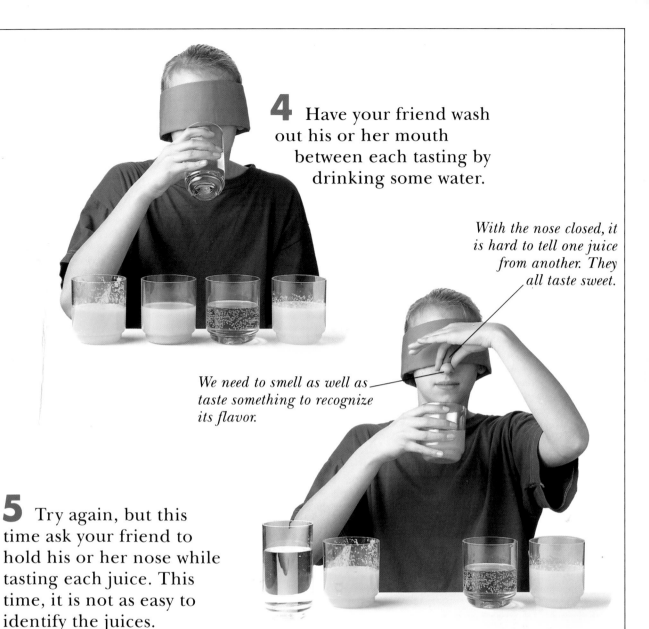

4 Have your friend wash out his or her mouth between each tasting by drinking some water.

With the nose closed, it is hard to tell one juice from another. They all taste sweet.

We need to smell as well as taste something to recognize its flavor.

5 Try again, but this time ask your friend to hold his or her nose while tasting each juice. This time, it is not as easy to identify the juices.

A meal without appeal

Food does not taste very good when you have a cold. This is not just because you are feeling ill—you probably have a stuffed-up nose as well. Your food seems to lose its flavor because you cannot smell it as easily as when you are healthy.

Taste test

Bake some good- and bad-tasting cookies, and find out how tiny bumps on your tongue, called taste buds, help you to detect basic tastes.

You will need:

Cookie sheet

 Mustard powder

 Salt

 Sugar

 Plain flour

 Tablespoon

Grated lemon peel

 Margarine

Paper towel

Rolling pin

Cutting board

Cookie cutter

 Food coloring

Four bowls

Flour and sugar

Flour and lemon peel

Flour and salt

Flour and mustard

1 In each bowl, mix two tablespoons of flour with a tablespoon of either sugar, salt, mustard powder, or lemon peel.

2 Add a tablespoon of margarine to each bowl and mix with your fingers.

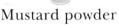

Wash your hands after mixing each bowl.

3 Add a different food coloring to three of the mixtures. Leave one mixture as it is.

4 Sprinkle flour on the cutting board. Roll out each mixture and cut out some cookies.

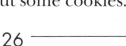

Wash the board, rolling pin, and cookie cutter between each mixture.

Grease the cookie sheet with a little margarine on a paper towel.

5 ⚠ Set the oven to 350° F (180° C). Put the cookies on the greased cookie sheet and bake them for 15 minutes.

Each taste— bitter (mustard), sour (lemon), salty, and sweet —is detected by a different part of your tongue.

6 ⚠ Using pot holders, take the cookie sheet out of the oven. Let the cookies cool, then taste one of each color. Rinse your mouth out with water after tasting each cookie.

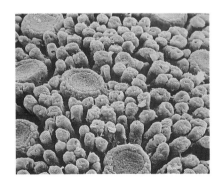

Taste detectors
This is a magnified view of the taste buds on your tongue. Different flavors are more easily detected on different areas of the tongue. You taste saltiness at the front, bitterness at the back, sourness at the sides, and sweetness over nearly all of it.

Potpourri

When we inhale, detectors in our noses smell different odors. Make a potpourri and create a sweet-smelling blend of different scents.

You will need:

Paper towels

Roses

Teaspoon

Saucer

Jar with lid

Cloves

Saucer

Cookie sheet

Cinnamon   Lavender   Mint

The mint and roses will dry in two to three days.

1 Line the cookie sheet with a paper towel and cover it with rose petals and mint. Put the cookie sheet in a warm, dry place.

2 Place the dried mint and rose petals in the jar. Add the lavender and a teaspoon of cinnamon.

3 Put the cloves in the saucer and crush them with the back of the spoon.

4 Add the crushed cloves to the jar. Twist the lid on and shake it well. This is your potpourri.

Put your potpourri in a bowl and let its scent fill the room.

5 Pour the potpourri into a bowl. Its scent is a blend of flowers and spices.

Swell smell

Many flowers have pleasant scents that attract flying insects, such as bees. The insects carry pollen from one flower to another. The plants need the pollen to produce seeds.

Picture credits
(Picture credits abbreviation key: B=below, C=center, L=left, R=right, T=top)

Lupe Cuhna Photo Library/Vaughan Melzer: 6BR; Robert Harding Picture Library/Photri: 19BR; The Image Bank Schmid/Langsfeld: 25BR; David Redfern Photography: 6BL; David Redfern Photography/Thomas Meyer: 13BR; Science Photo Library/Biofoto Associates: 9BL; Science Photo Library/ Dr Jeremy Burgess: 29BR; Science Photo Library/Omikron: 27BL; Zefa Picture Library: 15BL; Zefa Picture Library/K. Scholz: 7TR.

Picture research Kathy Lockley and Clive Webster

Science consultant Jack Challoner

Dorling Kindersley would like to thank Jenny Vaughan for editorial assistance; Mr Halpin, the staff and children of Harris City Technology College, London, especially Chad Calderbank, Andrea Charles, Elizabeth Dyer, Joel Edwards, Kristy Gould, James Jenkins, Chelene Jess, Amy Kelly, Faye Kester, Joanne McShane, Zoe Rooke, Raj Sudra, Emma White, Hing-Wai Wong, Sonia Opong, and Ben Sells.